OUR AMAZING WORLD

WHALES

Kay de Silva

Aurora

Contents

A Humpback Whale mom and baby swimming through tropical waters.

WHALES

Whales are big animals that live in the oceans. Whales are mammals, not fish. Whales are even bigger than dinosaurs.

A NATOMY

Blue Whales are known as the largest animals to have ever lived on earth. They can be 100 feet (30.5 meters) long and weigh 100 tons (101.6 tonnes). This equals the weight of about 23 elephants. Their tongues alone weigh as much as an elephant.

A deep-sea diver looks tiny next to the awesome Blue Whale.

A Killer Whale pod traveling in the wild.

MIGRATION

Whales live in oceans around the world. During winter, whales go from cold to warmer parts of the ocean. They have a thick layer of fat under their skins. The fat is called blubber and helps them to keep warm.

A Fin Whale breathing out.

BREATHING

Whales breathe air. They do not have gills like fish. They come up to the top of the ocean to get air. They use a blowhole found on the top of their heads to draw air in. Whales cannot sleep for more than 90 minutes at a time because they need to come up for air.

An Orca Whale, also known as a Killer Whale, showing off its teeth.

TOOTHED WHALES

Some whales have teeth. Others have baleen. *Toothed Whales* feed on small fish such as salmon, tuna, cod, and small mammals.

Orca Whales, also known as *Killer Whales*, are Toothed Whales. They are known as the *Wolves of the Sea*. They eat fish, dolphins, seals, and even Blue Whales.

A Grey Whale's baleen.

BALEEN WHALES

Baleen Whales have a row of plates on their upper jaws. The baleen looks like the teeth of a comb. Baleen Whales feed on plankton (a sea plant) and krill (a small, shrimp-like creature).

Baleen Whales are much larger than Toothed Whales. They have 2 blowholes instead of one.

WHALE SONG

Whales are noisy animals. They are the loudest animals in the world. They sigh, moan, groan, and speak to each other. These sounds travel very far across the ocean.

A whale's haunting melody travels long distances.

A family of Orca Whales.

WHALE FAMILIES

Whales live in large groups called *herds*. Mother whales are called *cows*. Father whales are called *bulls*. Baby whales are called *calves*. A whale calf grows inside its mother before it is born.

A Suckling baby Beluga.

BABY WHALES

Whale calves drink their mother's milk. The milk is full of fat and is as thick as toothpaste. The mother squirts the milk into the calf's mouth.

PLAY

Whales are playful animals. They can swim very fast. They also love to leap through the water into the air. This is called *breaching*.

A forty-foot long Humpback Whale having a whale of a time.

BLUE WHALES

Blue Whales are the largest animals in the world. They get their name from their bluish-grey skin color. Blue Whales eat mostly krill. During the feeding season one Blue Whale captures about 40 million krill every day.

Baby Blue Whales drink about 50 gallons of their mother's milk. Blue Whales off the coast of Sri Lanka are known to make songs of four notes. These songs last about 2 minutes each.

A glimpse of a magnificent Blue Whale.

The "hard-hat worker with a smile on its face."

BELUGA WHALES

Beluga Whales are dark grey when they are born. Their color fades over time. They are snow white as adults.

Beluga Whales look gentle, but do not let their smiles fool you. These Toothed Whales are carnivores, which means they eat other animals. They will eat any sea creature that is smaller than themselves.

The Fin Whale gets its name from the curved fin located far down its back.

FIN WHALES

Fin Whales are the second largest animal after the Blue Whale. They grow to nearly 88 feet (27 meters) long. They have slender bodies. They are called the *Greyhounds of the Sea*, because of their slim build and high speed when hunting.

Fin Whales can get 20 pounds (9 kilograms) of krill in a single gulp. They can gulp as often as every 30 seconds.

GREY WHALES

Grey Whales are medium-sized and grow to as large as 45 feet (13 meters) long. They are grey with white patches of parasites (barnacles and lice). They feed differently from other whales. These whales stir up shallow coastal areas and suck up small animals from the bottom.

Grey Whales have one of the longest migrations of all mammals. They live in the Arctic during the summer and travel to California as it gets cold.

Above: a Grey Whale in full flight.
Below: a breaching Grey Whale sequence.

HUMPBACK WHALES

Humpback Whales feed in groups. This is known as lunge feeding or bubble-net feeding. The whales work as a team to catch large schools of herring (a type of fish). Each team member has a job. Some blow bubbles around the fish to stop them from escaping. Others vocalize to scare the fish and bring them to the top. Others herd the fish. Then the whales open their mouths wide and gulp as many fish as they can.

Teamwork: Humpback Whales feeding.

A lone Minke Whale gliding through the water.

MINKE WHALES

Minke Whales are one of the smallest Baleen Whales; only the *Pygmy Right Whales* are smaller.

Minke Whales are black or dark grey. They have a white band on each of their flippers. Unlike most whales that live in herds, Minke Whales are shy. They like to live alone.

A herd of Narwhales—notice the male's tusk.

NARWHAL WHALES

Narwhals or Narwhales are medium-sized Toothed Whales. Narwhal males have a long, straight tusk that extends from their upper left jaw. The tusk is actually an overgrown tooth. It grows out of a hole in the whale's upper lip. No one knows why Narwhales have a tusk, as it does not seem to have a purpose.

ORCA WHALES

Orca or Killer Whales are known to be the fastest marine mammal. They can swim over 30mph (miles per hour) and about 75 miles a day. Orca Whale families are called *pods*.

These Whales are very protective of their calves. Young female whales in the pod help the mothers to care for their newborns.

A Killer Whale breaching near the Canadian coast.

SPERM WHALES

Sperm Whales are the largest Toothed Whales alive. They are able to dive deeper than any other whale. They dive over 3,280 feet (1,000 meters) and spend most of their time underwater. They find most of their food near the ocean floor.

The clicking vocalizations of Sperm Whales are the loudest sound made by any animal.

A lumbering Sperm Whale.

Two Humpback Whales and a shark swimming through ancient ruins.

PROTECT THE WHALES

Sadly, some species of whales, such as Humpback Whales, are in danger of becoming extinct. We must do our part by taking care of our environment to protect these amazing animals.

OUR AMAZING WORLD

COLLECT THEM ALL

WWW.OURAMAZINGWORLDBOOKS.COM

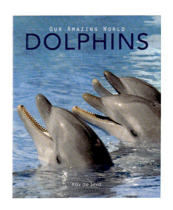

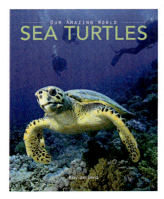

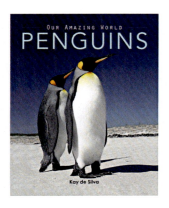

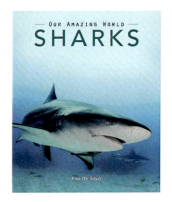

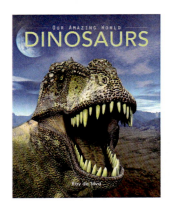

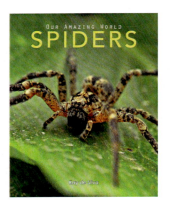

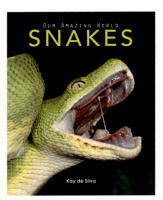

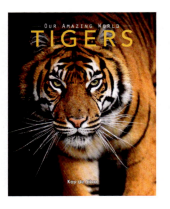

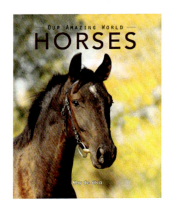

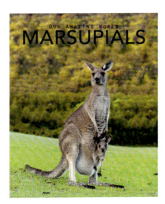

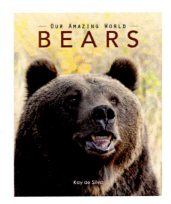

Aurora
An imprint of CKTY Publishing Solutions

www.ouramazingworldbooks.com

66183899R00020

Made in the USA
San Bernardino, CA
09 January 2018